SandCastle

Rhyme Time

Dwight and the Magic Kite

Tracy Kompelien

Consulting Editor, Diane Craig, M.A./Reading Specialist

ABDO
Publishing Company

Published by ABDO Publishing Company, 4940 Viking Drive, Edina, Minnesota 55435.

Printed in the United States.

Credits
Edited by: Pam Price
Curriculum Coordinator: Nancy Tuminelly
Cover and Interior Design and Production: Mighty Media
Photo and Illustration Credits: BananaStock Ltd., Comstock, Corbis Images, Digital Vision, Hemera, Image Source, ImageState, Tracy Kompelien, PhotoDisc, Stockbyte

Library of Congress Cataloging-in-Publication Data

Kompelien, Tracy, 1975-
    Dwight and the magic kite / Tracy Kompelien.
        p. cm. -- (Rhyme time)
    Includes index.
    ISBN 1-59197-787-8 (hardcover)
    ISBN 1-59197-893-9 (paperback)
    1. English language--Rhyme--Juvenile literature. I. Title. II. Rhyme time (ABDO Publishing Company)

PE1517K6624 2005
808.1--dc22
                                                                        2004049039

SandCastle™ books are created by a professional team of educators, reading specialists, and content developers around five essential components that include phonemic awareness, phonics, vocabulary, text comprehension, and fluency. All books are written, reviewed, and leveled for guided reading, early intervention reading, and Accelerated Reader® programs and designed for use in shared, guided, and independent reading and writing activities to support a balanced approach to literacy instruction.

Let Us Know

After reading the book, SandCastle would like you to tell us your stories about reading. What is your favorite page? Was there something hard that you needed help with? Share the ups and downs of learning to read. We want to hear from you! To get posted on the ABDO Publishing Company Web site, send us e-mail at:

sandcastle@abdopub.com

SandCastle Level: Transitional

Words that rhyme do
not have to be spelled the
same. These words rhyme
with each other:

bite
night
quite
bright
height
tight
kite
white
light
write

Frida has a sandwich for lunch.

She takes a big **bite**.

Nina and Chris wear sunglasses because the sun is **bright**.

Tina and Gayle are flying a **kite**.

Eric is shorter than his sister,
Deborah.

They are not the same height.

Bobby could not **quite** reach the top of the fence.

Dani's scarf is made out of
yellow feathers.

It is very light.

Laura likes to ice skate.

Her ice skates are white.

Sara's mom tucks her in at night.

Brent thinks about what to write.

When Jon gets a piggyback
ride, he holds on **tight**.

Dwight and the Magic Kite

Dwight dreamed one night
of a magic kite.

Though there was no wind in sight,
the kite started to take flight.

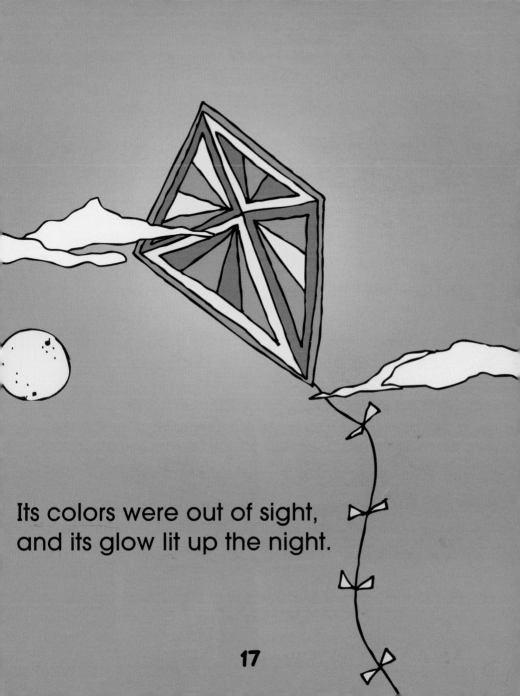

Its colors were out of sight,
and its glow lit up the night.

17

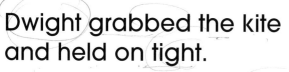

Dwight grabbed the kite
and held on tight.

As they rose to great height,
Dwight squealed with delight.

18

Suddenly, the light from the kite was no longer bright.

It was as dark as midnight.

What a terrible fright!

19

Dwight let go of that kite.

He was still in bed,
tucked in tight.

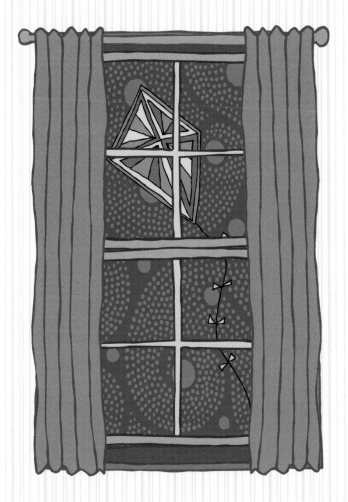

He fell back to sleep
knowing he was all right.

Rhyming Riddle

What do you call
a snack eaten after dark?

Night bite

Glossary

delight. great joy or happiness

ice skate. a boot with a metal blade attached to the bottom, used for gliding on ice

kite. a lightweight frame covered with paper or fabric that is flown at the end of a long string

magic. having strange or mysterious powers or qualities

piggyback. carried on the back or shoulders

quite. completely

About SandCastle™

A professional team of educators, reading specialists, and content developers created the SandCastle™ series to support young readers as they develop reading skills and strategies and increase their general knowledge. The SandCastle™ series has four levels that correspond to early literacy development in young children. The levels are provided to help teachers and parents select the appropriate books for young readers.

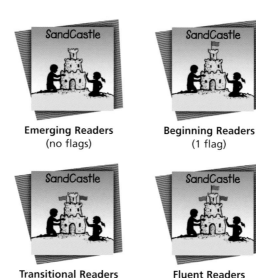

Emerging Readers
(no flags)

Beginning Readers
(1 flag)

Transitional Readers
(2 flags)

Fluent Readers
(3 flags)

These levels are meant only as a guide. All levels are subject to change.

To see a complete list of SandCastle™ books and other nonfiction titles from ABDO Publishing Company, visit www.abdopub.com or contact us at:
4940 Viking Drive, Edina, Minnesota 55435 • 1-800-800-1312 • fax: 1-952-831-1632